# Can You Trust Your Patent Attorney?

## 27 Questions You Must Ask Before Revealing Your Idea to (Or Hiring) Legal Counsel

by Rob Gramer

**Warning-Disclaimer:** I wrote this report to provide information in regard to the subject matter covered. It is offered with the understanding that the publisher and the author are not liable for the misconception or misuse of the information provided.
Every effort has been made to make this report as complete and accurate as possible. The purpose of this report is to educate. The author and the publisher shall have neither liability nor responsibility to any person or entity with respect to any loss, damage, or injury caused or alleged to be caused directly or indirectly by the information contained in this report. No offer of investment is being made. The information presented herein is in no way intended as a substitute for legal counseling.

Go to www.inventionprep.com to learn how to start profiting off your idea in the next 30 days.

# Can You Trust Your Patent Attorney?

## 27 Questions You Must Ask Before Revealing Your Idea to (or Hiring) a Patent Attorney

You have an idea that could be worth millions (or billions).

And you want to protect this idea with a patent.

So, you've decided that you want to sit down with a patent attorney to discuss your idea...see if it qualifies for a patent...and possibly hire him to write the patent application for you.

But, how do you know this person isn't going to run off with your idea and keep it for themselves?

How do you know they won't tell someone else?

How do you know this person isn't going to overcharge you (or "hide" fees so you don't know how much the entire process costs)?

How do you know this person is even qualified to write a good application?

In essence, how do you know you can trust them?

---

Go to www.inventionprep.com to learn how to start profiting off your idea in the next 30 days.

This book aims to answer those question.

In fact, this book will tell you the 27 questions you must ask a patent attorney before you reveal your idea...AND...the how they must answer them to gain your trust.

### How Do I Know What You Should Ask?

My name is Rob Gramer. For two years I worked for a pair of patent attorneys. My job was to talk to inventors...determine if their idea was something possible and qualified for protection (my background is in mechanical engineering)...and then help put together the documentation necessary for the attorneys to draft the patent application.

During this time, thousands of inventions were submitted to our office. And through my conversations with inventors I heard tons of horror stories.

A few:

A medical device company was selling millions of dollars worth of a patented product. Because of a misspelling of one word by a SINGLE LETTER, the entire patent was invalid and competition flooded the market, costing the company millions.

Another inventor was "firing" his previous patent attorney. After spending $15,000 for the patent application, the patent attorney failed to tell the inventor of ongoing fees (to the tune of $5,000 and

Go to www.inventionprep.com to learn how to start profiting off your idea in the next 30 days.

growing) for office action responses and other work the patent office required.

Another inventor lost protection for his idea because his patent attorney failed to remind the inventor of maintenance fees for the issued patent. When the company he was licensing his idea to got wind, they promptly cancelled the agreement - costing the inventor five figures a month.

And on and on...

From those conversations, and the questions people asked me, I put together this list of 27 questions.

This book is pretty simple. First, I list the question you must ask. Second, is what the attorney should say to answer the question properly. If they can't answer the question, there's a good chance there is something fishy about them.

Sound simple enough?

Ok, good. This book is short so you should be able to read it in one sitting. My hope is that you'll use the information here to make sure you are dealing with a reputable and trustworthy patent attorney.

Let's begin...

Go to www.inventionprep.com to learn how to start profiting off your idea in the next 30 days.

**Question #1: How do I know you are not going to steal my idea?**

*The reason why you ask this question is simple, you want to make sure the person you are talking to is not going to run off with your idea. Here are the 7 reasons you want to hear.*

Reasons #1: <u>Your confidentiality is guaranteed by federal law</u>. As Registered Patent Attorneys, our firm is licensed to practice before the United States Patent & Trademark Office and is legally bound by Title 37 of the Code of Federal Regulations (Section 10.57) to maintain the strictest confidentiality with respect to invention submissions.

All patent attorneys are covered by this code of federal regulations.

Reason #2: Our track record of maintaining secrecy. We've been registered with the Patent Office since (insert year here). Since that time there has been <u>ZERO complaints filed against us or our firm</u>. We adhere to the strictest secrecy and confidentiality requirements.

If they don't have zero strikes against them, beware!

Reason #3: Demonstrated Intellectual Property Law expertise. We are <u>Board Certified by the (State) Bar as an expert in Intellectual Property Law</u>. Certification is the highest level of recognition of the competency

Go to www.inventionprep.com to learn how to start profiting off your idea in the next 30 days.

and experience of attorneys approved for certification by the State Supreme Court.

This is extra certification that the attorney you are dealing with is certified an expert by the state.

Reason #4: Before disclosing any sensitive information to us, we will provide you with a signed Confidentiality Agreement. This means you will have a written record of disclosing your idea to us.

NEVER tell anyone your idea if they will not sign a confidentiality agreement.

Reason #5: Technical expertise. Along with being Registered Patent Attorneys, we hold technical degrees.

Any patent attorney also has to have a bachelors of science degree. If you have a chemical invention, you're better off dealing with a patent attorney who has a chemical background. Find out their schooling to make sure they are even more qualified to handle your idea.

Reason #6: Your idea is in the hands of specialists. We are not a "jack of all trades" firm. We do not handle speeding tickets, divorces, or personal injury. We focus 100% on Intellectual Property Law, making sure your idea is protected.

Do you really want a patent attorney who moonlights fighting speeding tickets? Of course not. Make sure

Go to www.inventionprep.com to learn how to start profiting off your idea in the next 30 days.

the attorney you are dealing with exclusively handles intellectual property law.

Reason #7: <u>Other lawyers rank us in the top 3%</u>. Our firm has been awarded an AV rating, the highest rating possible by the Martindale-Hubbell Law Directory for our legal expertise and overall professional excellence. This is a peer rating award, meaning that our peers rank us at the highest level of professional excellence.

An AV rating is a peer rating meaning the law firm is highly regarded by other lawyers. This is a green light to deal with this attorney.

*When it comes to these reasons, the more the better. If the attorney you are dealing with cannot answer they questions like the answers I provided, be wary of how secure your idea will be with them.*

Go to www.inventionprep.com to learn how to start profiting off your idea in the next 30 days.

**Question #2: What's the risk I run by telling someone my idea without patenting it?**

*This is a "qualifying" question. You want to make sure the attorney is accurately explains the pros and cons of going through the patenting process.*

The short answer is, it could get stolen. There are no laws in the United States against blatantly copying ideas or products. A patent is the only way to get a "legal monopoly" on your idea. This gives you the sole right to make, manufacture, or sell your invention. If anyone else wants this right they usually have to pay you for that permission in the form of royalties or licensing fees.

Beware of any attorney who tries to scare you with hype...that there are "sharks" out there just waiting to prey on new inventors who put their products on the market.

Yes, people steal ideas all the time. But most experienced business people will wait to see if the idea takes off before stealing it. Not too many people are interested in an unproven idea.

Go to www.inventionprep.com to learn how to start profiting off your idea in the next 30 days.

**Question #3: How much does a patent cost?**

*Make sure the patent attorney explains your different options...INCLUDING ongoing costs (such as application fees, fees for responding to patent office responses, and maintenance fees). These fees can come into play YEARS after you first sit down with the attorney. The last thing you want is more and more bills appearing in your mailbox without you expecting them.*

Depending on what route you take a patent can cost you a few hundred bucks or tens of thousands. Let's look at the options you have, what they will run you in out-of-pocket expenses, and the pros and cons involved with each one.

At the bare minimum are the government filing fees involved with submitting a patent application. Currently the fees start at about $125 and go up to $530 depending on what type of application you submit. If you do all the work yourself of drafting the application and drawings, this is all you will pay to get your application in and to "patent pending" status.

Warning: just because you submit something does not necessarily mean your idea is protected. Only when your application is drafted properly, and contain all the "elements" required by the patent office, are you fully protected. The "quantity" of protection you get is directly related to the "quality" of the application

Go to www.inventionprep.com to learn how to start profiting off your idea in the next 30 days.

submitted. (We'll talk more about this in a moment.)

However, if you either cannot or do not wish to draft the application then you'll have to get someone to do it for you. Usually, this means hiring a patent attorney.

We generally charge between $3,000 and $30,000 (*this is a FAIR range for most applications*) for the patent application depending on the scope of your invention.

However, this is just the fee for us to draft the application. There are other fees such as:

Responding to office actions: $500 to $3,000 plus patent office fees

Note: you can find any patent fees on the United States Patent and Trademark Office website at www.uspto.gov.

Go to www.inventionprep.com to learn how to start profiting off your idea in the next 30 days.

## Question #4: How do I know you are competitively priced?

*There is no set price for an attorney to charge you for drafting a patent. However, some patent attorneys will use the following line of reasoning when justifying their price. If an attorney gives you this explanation, it usually means they understand the detail that goes into the application (which is a good sign). Also, you may want to ask if they take place in an annual internal audit of patent attorneys fees.*

Every year we take place in an annual internal audit of fees charged by patent attorneys. While we are not on the lower end of the scale, we are competitively priced among attorneys with similar experience and technical knowledge.

Bottom line: we will always quote you a fair price for drafting your patent application. Anyone who quotes lower than us generally does not have the same level of experience as we do.

Either way, thousands of dollars in fees brings up the question...Why would you pay somebody thousands or even tens of thousands of dollars when you can do it yourself?

The #1 reason is because, failure to draft the application properly results in less protection (or no protection) for your idea. Why? Because patents are property. And as with any other type of property law

Go to www.inventionprep.com to learn how to start profiting off your idea in the next 30 days.

you only get coverage for the scope of the property included in the application that you submit to the governing body. In this case of patents, you use words, sentences, and paragraphs to define what your idea is.

Let's use an analogy of physical property to make this easier to understand.

When you buy a parcel of land you have a surveyor come out and measures the amount of property purchased. The surveyor then records this on a piece of paper and submit this application to a governing body (usually a city or county government). Whatever he records on this piece of paper - as far as the governing body is concerned - is what you own.

Now let's imagine this surveyor is horrible at his job. You have just bought an acre of land, but the surveyor instead records you only bought half an acre, which he writes down on the application he submits it to the governing body. Well, guess what happens? As far as the governing body is concerned, you do not own an acre of land...you only own HALF an acre of land. And if your new friendly neighbor claims the land that the surveyor omitted from the application, well, you're going to be in for one heck of a legal battle.. because of mistake by the surveyor!

The key here is, when it comes to property law you only get what you ask for in the application.

That is why it's so important to make sure you properly define your invention in the application according to the specifications laid out by the patent office! Fail to do this and you risk getting full protection for your idea.

So how does this apply to inventions and patents?

Imagine you've invented a time machine. And your first prototype is made of wood...two by fours, plywood, and other scrap you had lying around. Well if you drafted up at an application describing a device that travels back in time and is made of wood, then that is what you would get protection for. A time machine made of wood.

However, the important aspect of this invention is not that it's made of wood. No, the importance of your machine is the fact it travels back in time (regardless of the material it is made of)!

The proper way to drop the application would be to leave out the fact that it was made out of wood and just talk about the fact that it travels back in time. But, if you made the mistake of include the fact that it's made out of wood, somebody else can come out the market build a time machine made out of metal and not necessarily infringe upon your idea.

The fact of the matter is you do not want to include extraneous details about your invention into the application. You only want to argue in the application why your idea qualifies for a patent. You don't need to talk about all these other things, engineering or manufacturing other parts, and so on.

Patents only deal with the LEGAL side of inventions...so you must stick to only a legal argument in the application.

If you do not you could risk getting full protection for your idea, or you can give somebody a way to get around your invention. This is the reason why it makes sense to hire somebody who knows what they're doing.

Going back to our Time Machine example, imagine how much the time machine would be worth out in the open market. Millions, billions, as much - and more - money as you possibly think. But if you didn't have the patent drafted properly, if you only have "protection for one made out of wood, not metal or other material" other people can build it and you would lose out on a lot of those potential profits.

If your invention is truly worth millions of dollars (or even just a few hundreds of thousands of dollars) over the course of the 20 year life of the patent, then why wouldn't you spend $5,000 $10,000 $15,000 or more to have it done properly?

Go to www.inventionprep.com to learn how to start profiting off your idea in the next 30 days.

**Question #5: Do you charge for your initial consultation?**

*Some do, some don't. But make sure you know up front. The last thing you want is to sit down with an attorney and then be hit with a big bill you didn't know was coming. Also, ask if the consultation price is paid forward towards any future work.*

Go to www.inventionprep.com to learn how to start profiting off your idea in the next 30 days.

## Question #6: How long does it take to get the application submitted?

*This is an important question because as soon as the application is submitted, you are at the patent pending. This means you have a date on file with the patent office, and can now reveal your idea and still have a level of protection. Make sure you nail down how long it will take them to get you to this point.*

The real questions there is, how long does it take to draft an application? The direct answer is 3 – 8 weeks. How long it will take to draft your application depends on 3 factors.

1.    What category does your idea fall into?

2.    How complex is it?

3.    How similar is it to other "stuff" that is already out there?

Let's take a closer look at these three:

Category – is your idea mechanical, electrical, chemical, biotech, a business concept, software based, or a combination of a few of these? An easier category generally means a quicker turnaround time.

For example, it would be quick to draft a patent application for a paper clip. Not so quick for a space shuttle.

Complexity – obviously, the more complex your idea, the longer it will take to draft the patent application.

Similarity – part of the patent application process is defining how different your idea is from other things that are out there. For example, I know from experience there are thousands of patents on different baby feeding bottles. So if you come up with an idea for a new one, it's not just defining how yours works, a good patent will also define how it is different from the thousands of other patents out there. Obviously, this could not only take some time, but also drive up the price of the patent.

Go to www.inventionprep.com to learn how to start profiting off your idea in the next 30 days.

## Question #7: What does patent pending mean?

*You want to make sure the patent attorney can explain what level of protection you are at and what your future obligations are.*

At the point you are as legally protected as you can possibly be without getting the actual patent itself. In other words, get your product out there…market it, license it, sell it, whatever. Just go make some money!

But do NOT do it before you get that patent pending status.

To get there, you must submit an application (either a provisional patent application or a non provisional patent application) to the United State Patent and Trademark Office (USPTO). When you submit an application, the USPTO gives you a receipt that states the patent application number and the date it was submitted. This is your filing date and you are "patent pending". Generally, it takes us 3-8 weeks to draft a patent application, depending on the scope of your idea.

Go to www.inventionprep.com to learn how to start profiting off your idea in the next 30 days.

## Question #8: How long does a patent last?

*Make sure the attorney explains how long your patent lasts and what your obligations are for the life of the patent.*

It depends on what type of patent you apply for.

A design patent expires after 14 years. There are two ways to apply for a utility patent. The provisional patent covers you for one year. A non provisional patent lasts 20 years. (Note: you can convert your provisional patent application into the full 20 year non provisional patent if you finish the application before the one year time limit is up.)

During the time period you own the patent, you are the only one who can manufacture, market, or sell the idea. If anyone else wants to introduce your patented idea into the marketplace, they must ask for your permission (which usually means paying you) before they can do so.

After these time frames are up, your patent then goes into the public domain and you no longer have exclusive rights to use the idea and anyone can use it without asking you.

Go to www.inventionprep.com to learn how to start profiting off your idea in the next 30 days.

## Question #9: Why do I need a patent?

*Here the patent attorney should be able to explain the benefits of getting a patent.*

How would you feel if you saw your product on stores shelves across the country and someone else was getting rich (and you weren't seeing a penny)? Or what would go through your mind if you slaved away developing a product over the span of a few years, only to have someone copy your design outright? What if a friend stole your idea and sold it to a competitor?

If any of these situations would make your blood boil, well, that's why you need a patent.

Without a patent, there is nothing stopping anybody from outright stealing the idea from you...copying it piece by piece...selling it...and directly competing with you for market share.

A patent protects your hard work and ingenuity. You need a patent because it gives you **ownership** of your idea. No one else can manufacture, market or sell something that is related to your idea without your (usually paid for) permission. It's like having a title to a car, or a title to a house. A title says you own that car or that house. A patent is title to intellectual property.

In a nutshell, a patent gives you a legal monopoly on your idea. If anybody else wants to use it, they must

Go to www.inventionprep.com to learn how to start profiting off your idea in the next 30 days.

pay you for that privilege.

Go to www.inventionprep.com to learn how to
start profiting off your idea in the next 30 days.

## Question #10: How much does a patent search cost and how long does it take?

*A patent search is research done to see if your idea is already out there. If it is, in many cases, this prevents you from getting protection for your idea. This process can save you from wasting lots of time and money. But you don't want to be overcharged for it.*

The answer to both of those questions really depend on the scope of your invention. However, a good rule of thumb is anywhere from $500 to $3,000 and 7-10 business days. Keep in mind, we've completed patent searches in a few days. And sometimes we want to "dig a little deeper" and may need a few extra days.

Where your patent search falls in the $500 to $3,000 dollar range depends on the scope of your idea. Factors like category, complexity, how many other products are similar to your invention (and a few other factors) determine the fee for the patent search. Once we know exactly what your invention is and how it works - which is discussed during the free consultation - we can provide you with a fixed fee quote for the search.

But whatever the fee and time frame, you must get one additional thing when you have a patent search done for you. It is an important legal document that ensures a thorough and complete search was conducted. If you do not insist on this document, you'll

Go to www.inventionprep.com to learn how to start profiting off your idea in the next 30 days.

have no recourse if the researcher "misses" something. And you'll have wasted thousands of dollars and months (sometimes years) pursuing an idea that can not be protected.

And that document is a written legal opinion.

Whenever we do a search we always provide you with a written legal opinion letter on the patentability of your invention. Keep in mind that not all law firms will provide a written legal opinion. The reason for this is liability.

It is sort of like when you go to a doctor. Imagine if - after going in for a routine checkup - you left with a clean bill of health. And then imagine a week later you found out you had full blown stage four cancer. Shouldn't the doctor have found it?

In this case you can actually sue the doctor for malpractice for missing the cancer.

It works the same way for us. When we do a search, we have a legal responsibility to be as thorough as possible. If we miss something, and give you a green light in the opinion letter, we are committing legal malpractice, and you can come after us. That is a big reason why many law firms refuse to give you a patent search opinion in writing. They want to be able to "deny" they ever gave you a green light. If you have a written legal opinion, signed by an attorney, it is very difficult to deny that in a court of law.

Go to www.inventionprep.com to learn how to start profiting off your idea in the next 30 days.

So, make sure you always get a written legal opinion on your patent search.

This brings me to my second point. What happens if you hire someone to do a search, and then your patent application gets rejected because the person doing the research missed something?

Well, if it was a registered Patent Attorney, you can sue them. But that is not the case if they are not registered. There are a lot of people who are "researchers" (whatever that means), who are willing to do a patent search for what seems like a lot less money. However, these people are rarely ever patent agents or patent attorneys. By the way, this is who usually does the research when you go to one of those "inventor help" type companies. In this case, it is unlawful for them to give you a legal opinion (how can they, they are not lawyers!) If the researcher misses something during their search, you have no legal recourse whatsoever

Imagine going through the application process, spending thousands of dollars on drafting the application...and months (sometimes years) waiting to hear back from the patent office...only to find out your application was rejected because the researcher missed something.

It may be a little bit more expensive up front, but this is why it pays to hire someone to do it right! You do

Go to www.inventionprep.com to learn how to start profiting off your idea in the next 30 days.

not want to throw good money after bad, investing thousands of dollars and hundreds of hours putting together an idea that someone else owns!

Go to www.inventionprep.com to learn how to start profiting off your idea in the next 30 days.

## Question #11: What IS a patent?

*Before going down this road of getting protection for your idea, it's important to know exactly what a patent is.*

A patent is title to intellectual property. It signifies ownership of an invention, idea, or method.

This can be a little difficult to understand. So let's take a closer look at intellectual property law.

Intellectual property law works much like real property law works. It is much easier to think about tangible items (like real property...cars, houses, clothes, etc.) than it is to think about intangible items (like inventions, ideas, and methods), so let's use an example from physical property law to define patents.

Suppose you buy a house. When you buy this house you get a title to the house. The title has your name on it, your social security number, the property address and so on and so forth. This document - the title - ties you to the property and signifies ownership.

The same thing happens when you buy a car. You get a title to the car and it has your name, social security number, and the vehicle identification number on it as well. This ties you to the vehicle.

Well, a patent is the exact same thing. The patent has your name on it, your social security number on it, and a description of the idea.

Go to www.inventionprep.com to learn how to start profiting off your idea in the next 30 days.

Now the big difference between cars and houses is that patents are intellectual property. This means you must use words and sentences and paragraphs to describe what the intellectual property is. The danger here is that if you use the wrong words and sentences and paragraphs you may not get protection for your idea.

Let's see just how wrong this can go. Going back to our example about physical property. When you buy a house a person called a surveyor comes out and surveys your property. What he does is he writes down on a piece of paper how much land you own. He then submits this piece of paper to a governing body. As far as the governing body is concerned, whatever is written down on that piece of paper is how much land you own.

Makes sense, right?

Well, let's say you bought an acre of land, but the surveyor doesn't do a very good job. And instead of writing down that you own one acre of land, he writes down that you own HALF an acre of land. Well guess what! If he submits that piece of paper to the governing body, as far as that governing body is concerned you do not own an acre of land. Oh no, you only own HALF an acre of land!

This is why it is so important to get proper documentation! God forbid you buy a Ferrari, but the

Go to www.inventionprep.com to learn how to start profiting off your idea in the next 30 days.

title you are given has the vehicle identification number for a Ford.

That is why it is so important to hire someone who knows what they are doing. If you fail to properly draft the patent application, you may be putting your property at risk.

### Question #12: What can be and what can't be patented?

*Make sure your patent attorney can explain the basic qualifying rules for an invention.*

To answer this question let's first talk about what the patent office requires when you file an application.

The patent office requires 3 things. They want an application, which is a written description of what your invention is. They want drawings, which are a visual description of what your invention is. And they want their government application fee to cover reviewing your invention to determine whether or not it applies for patent protection or not.

What this means is that they do not need a business plan. They do not need a prototype or a working model. They just need paper with drawings and words that describe what your invention its.

With those definitions in mind, let's take a look at a few of the criteria that must go in to the written patent application.

There are many of these but by far the biggies are, first, your invention must be new, so it can't be out there. And, second, it must be useful, which means it must serve some sort of benefit to the person using it. Keep in mind these are not all of the criteria. These are just the ones that are most important to think

Go to www.inventionprep.com to learn how to start profiting off your idea in the next 30 days.

about first.

So let's define those two words, new and useful.

New means that it has to be new. Not new in the United States. Not new in your industry. New. This is why it so important to do a patent search globally. The patent office will not give you a patent on something that's already been invented or in use in another country. It has to be new, period.

Usefu . This means it must serve some sort of benefit to the person that is using it. This can be a very broad definition. For example, if you drink coffee I'm sure you seen those little cardboard sleeves that go around the outside of coffee cups. Next time you get a cup of coffee take a close look on the sleeve and you'll notice a patent number on the outside.

How can you get a patent on something as simple as cardboard gluec around a cup? Simple, the usefulness. It serves a huge benefit! It prevents your fingers from getting burned while you're drinking the coffee.

This is #1 reason why we do not care too much about the "nuts and belts" of your invention. As long as it meets the criteria of being new and useful, you have a fighting chance of securing a patent. Even if it is something as common as cardboard and glue. If you manage to invent a device that serves a huge benefit like "preventing peoples fingers from getting burned

Go to www.inventionprep.com to learn how to
start profiting off your idea in the next 30 days.

while drinking a scalding hot liquid", it is possible to get a patent on something.

Go to www.inventionprep.com to learn how to start profiting off your idea in the next 30 days.

**Question #13: I hear terms like design patent, utility patent, provisional patent, and non provisional patent. What is the difference between all of these?**

*Depending on what you are trying to protect, you'll want to submit an application for a certain type of patent.*

There are two major types of patents, design and utility. The main differences is that a design patent protect the way something looks and a utility patent protect the way something works.

An example is in order.

Let's say you designed a new tie that was cut with a zigzag pattern in it. If you wanted to protect your unique design, you would file a design patent. Design patents protect the way something looks.

However let's say you develop a tie that extended all the way down to your waist and held your pants up. Now that would have a specific utility (hence the name utility), so you would protect it with a utility patent. Make sense, right?

A design patent is good for 14 years. The utility patent is good for 20 years.

Provisional and non-provisional are terms that describe the type of application you submit for a UTILITY patent. The easiest way to think about these

Go to www.inventionprep.com to learn how to start profiting off your idea in the next 30 days.

two applications is that the provisional patent application gives you protection for one year, and then expires, while the non provisional patent application submits your idea for consideration for the full 20 years of protection. You can always upgrade the provisional patent application to the non-provisional patent application. (In fact, most people I meet with apply for the 1 your provisional patent application first and then convert that to the full 20 year non provisional patent application later.)

An important note there is absolutely no difference whatsoever in the amount of protection you get between a provisional or the non provisional patent application. No matter what you submit, your idea is covered by the patent pending status while it is still in the application phase.

Go to www.inventionprep.com to learn how to start profiting off your idea in the next 30 days.

**Question #14: Why did someone else quote me a very low price for a provisional patent application?**

*You want to ask this question to make sure the person drafting your application is qualified to do so. Remember, a patent is a legal document...what you say is VERY important.*

Because the patent office doesn't ever review the provisional patent application. And if the person drafting your application (the one who gave you a low price) does a bad job, you'll never know until it is too late. But I'm getting ahead of myself.

There are many reasons people quote low for a provisional patent application.

Perhaps they are fresh out of law school and don't quite understand how much work goes into properly preparing an application. Maybe they lack experience and the only way they can get business is by charging less. Possibly they are just a filing service, and file whatever paperwork you give them whether it meets the requirements the patent office wants to see in an application or not.

Whatever the case, you need to understand how an improperly prepared provisional patent application can kill your chances of getting adequate protection for your idea.

Let's begin by defining what a provisional patent application is.

First, there is no such thing as a provisional patent. There is only a provisional patent application. A patent is what gives you legal protection for your idea. An application is what you fill out to apply for the patent. You may think I'm being nit-picky here, but you'll see why this is important in second.

The full patent application is broken up into two parts, the specifications section, and the claims section. When you submit a provisional patent application you are only submitting the specifications section.

Within the specifications, the USPTO requires - aside from just the background, summary, abstract, and detailed description of the invention - information about your invention like a title, cross-referencing any related applications, and a few other things.

Forget just one section here and the patent office could reject your application! And you won't discover this until YEARS after the provisional patent application was drafted.

Secondly, like I mentioned above, the USPTO does NOT review your provisional patent application. They simply record the date you submitted it (your patent pending date), and then wait until they get the full application to start the review process.

Go to www.inventionprep.com to learn how to start profiting off your idea in the next 30 days.

Hers is where you can royally get screwed...

Let's say you submitted your provisional patent application on July 4th, 2012. And you follow up with the non-provisional patent application within the one year time frame...February 10th, 2013. What happens next is the patent office reviews both applications to see how similar they are.

If there is a lot of ADDITIONAL information in the second application, you could risk losing your original filing date. This means your official patent date would NOT be July 4th, 2012, but instead it would be February 10th, 2013.

This may not be a huge problem, unless of course someone put a product like yours out in the market (or filed for a patent themselves) between July 4th, 2012 and February 10th, 2013. If that's the case, you may lose all rights to your invention.

This is why it is so important to submit a provisional patent application that meets all the requirements of the patent office and is not just an empty "placeholder". If you idea is not presented in the original provisional patent application, the patent office may accuse you of not having your idea fully thought out and you could get stuck with the later filing cate.

Go to www.inventionprep.com to learn how to start profiting off your idea in the next 30 days.

## Question #15: Why are costs so different from one firm to another?

*You not only want to know what an attorney charges, but also how they charge and when. This will prevent you from diving in with an attorney who seems "cheap" on the surface...but ends up costing you a lot in the long run.*

One of the reasons our quotes may differ from other firms is because we believe in disclosing any and all fees up front. Other places may leave out...

- Government filing fees
- Drawing fees
- Administrative fees
- Paralegal fees
- Response fees
- And other miscellaneous fees

...making the dollar amount appear much less. But in the end, the total cost of the patent would be very similar (or in some cases, much, much more). We believe it is only right to show you all of this up front.

Also, we will not lure you in with a ridiculously low price and then hit you with a huge bill later.

And yes, that does happen! Here's how...

Perhaps you've heard of the terms "non-provisional" and "provisional" patent application. In a nutshell, a non-provisional is for the full twenty year patent. A

Go to www.inventionprep.com to learn how to start profiting off your idea in the next 30 days.

provisional only protects you for one year. However, you can always "upgrade" the provisional to the full twenty year patent as long as you submit some paperwork before the year is up.

You must keep in mind the patent office NEVER reviews the provisional patent. It just acts as a placeholder until you upgrade to the full, non-provisional patent application.

Here's how the scam works.

An unscrupulous person will lure you in with a low-ball price for the one year, provisional patent. Usually, they will fail to mention the part where you have to convert it to the full, twenty year non-provisional patent application to get full protection. And then, when the one year patent is about to expire, they will call you up and - usually in a very urgent tone - explain how you must finish your patent application or risk losing rights to your idea!

That is when you'll get hit with a huge bill to finish the application up. And by that time, it's too late for you to research other avenues for finishing up your patent. You'll either have to fork up for their huge bill, or abandon the patent on your idea.

This is predatory behavior! Designed to put you in a vulnerable position and then bilk you dry. We do NOT operate this way, instead we will provide a written quote up front for the full non-provisional and

Go to www.inventionprep.com to learn how to start profiting off your idea in the next 30 days.

provisional patent application. This way you will know exactly how much every step of the patent application process will cost you...upfront...before you pay us one single penny.

Go to www.inventionprep.com to learn how to start profiting off your idea in the next 30 days.

## Question #16: How do you charge for your services?

*I recommend you find an attorney with the following approach. You'll know exactly what you are spending right out of the gate, instead of just getting bill after bill.*

First, the initial consultation is free. Next, we work on a fixed fee NOT an hourly basis. Most firms operate the exact opposite. This means they will draft your application and present a bill to you based on how many hours it took for them to draft it.

The problem with this approach is twofold. First, you have no clue how much it will cost you before you start. And second, what is stopping them from "fudging the numbers" and overbilling you by a few hours? How would you even know if they did?

The problem with billing on an hourly basis is you never know how much the entire process will cost before you get started. We ONLY work on a fixed fee basis. This means you will get a written quote - with all fees including our legal fees, drawing fees, and government filing fees - upfront. You will know what the entire application process costs, to the penny, before you get started.

Go to www.inventionprep.com to learn how to start profiting off your idea in the next 30 days.

## Question #17: Can't you just change a product 5 or 10 percent and get around the patent?

*This question is to make sure the attorney can explain to you how he is going to draft the patent to get you full protection. Make sure he gives you something like the following answer.*

The answer to that question depends on how well the actual patent is written.

If it is poorly written, and you have zero REAL protection (even if you do have an application number, or the actual patent itself) then anyone can copy you with reckless abandon and there is nothing you can do about it.

However, if it is written rock solid then there's no possible way to get around it.

Think about it like a bulletproof vest . You can put a vest on, but if it doesn't have the armor inside of it it isn't going to do you a whole lot of good.

A patent is only as good as the person who drafted it.

Here's what I mean by that last statement. A patent is only as good as the words, sentences, and paragraphs that are used to describe the invention. The question then isn't whether or not you can get around a patent, the question is in the skill of the person drafting the application.

Go to www.inventionprep.com to learn how to start profiting off your idea in the next 30 days.

Let's look at three ways you can mess up a patent application .

First, is by specifying dimensions of the product or parts of the product when they have nothing to do with the utility. Let's say you build a time machine, does it really matter if it is 5 feet tall or 20 feet tall? No, of course not! The only thing that matters is that I could travel back in time not how big or small it is. Never include the mansions in the patent application, or you could risk somebody else simply building something of a different size and getting around your patent.

Next, never call out the material of the device your building. Again let's use the imaginary example of a time machine. Suppose you built your time machine out of wood, two by fours and plywood, etc. Well, if in the patent application you specified your time machine was made out of wood, that is what you would get protection for a time machine made of wood. The problem here is that if somebody else build a time machine made of metal they are not infringing upon your patent because you specified it was "made out of wood". This is why you do not want to get so specific on how are what you make your invention out of, but rather talk about what it does.

Finally, and this is where a lot of inventors trip to up, you want to make sure that you explain parts of the device in a broad as possible terms. Let's say your

Go to www.inventionprep.com to learn how to start profiting off your idea in the next 30 days.

time machine worked because of a magnetic field. If you were to describe the inner workings of the time machine and say it contained magnets, then that is what you would own...a time machine with magnets inside .

But as anybody familiar with electricity knows, you can create a magnetic field by running electricity through a coiled wire. That means if someone were to build a time machine that did not have magnets in it but instead created the magnetic field with electricity and coil wire, then they would not be infringing upon your patent.

These are just a few examples of how things can go wrong in a patent application and leave you without protection (even though technically you have a patent). Remember, a patent is just a written document. Use the wrong words, sentences, and paragraphs to explain your idea and you may not get protection for parts, or even all, of your idea.

## Question #18: Can you work on royalties?

*Most patent attorneys will not work on a royalty basis.*

Go to www.inventionprep.com to learn how to start profiting off your idea in the next 30 days.

**Question #19: Should I hire an attorney who is local to me?**

*All patent applications are delivered to the United States Patent Office located in Alexandria, Virginia. Location of the attorney is not really a factor.*

If you were looking for a heart surgeon for an important operation, would you limit your search to those advertising in your local phone book or within driving distance?

Of course not. You would look for the most experienced, recommended, and qualified doctor you can find—and travel to him or her to have your operation.

Since hiring a patent attorney requires no travel, why limit your search to the closest attorneys you can find?

All patenting matters can (and usually are) handled by us via telephone, facsimile, email, and overnight delivery without any required in-person meetings. A significant number of my clients are located outside of Florida and many are even outside of the United States.

Today, most patent applications are filed ELECTRONICALLY over the Internet using the Patent Office's digital filing software—making a lawyer's distance from the Patent Office completely irrelevant.

Go to www.inventionprep.com to learn how to start profiting off your idea in the next 30 days.

In fact, the U.S. Patent Office stopped maintaining paper copies of patents at their patent search facility years ago.

Less than 1 percent of all lawyers are registered to practice before the United States Patent Office. Why limit your choice of a lawyer even further by focusing on the tiny handful of patent lawyers that happen to be within driving distance of you?

Go to www.inventionprep.com to learn how to start profiting off your idea in the next 30 days.

**Question #20: What is the difference between having a law firm do the work and having one of those "invention help" companies do it for me?**

*Make sure the attorney can explain what he brings to the table versus ever other option available to you.*

The main reason is because they are not law firms, and they are not governed by a code of ethics as we are. In fact, the United States Patent Office even warns consumers not to trust companies like this. You can see the USPTO warning here:

www.uspto.gov/web/offices/com/iip/documents/scamp revent.pdf

Secondly, you can't always be sure of their credentials. We've not only gone to law school, but we own technical degrees as well.

Even if you decide not to use us, we highly recommend you hire a registered patent attorney to draft your application for you.

Go to www.inventionprep.com to learn how to start profiting off your idea in the next 30 days.

## Question #21: What is the appointment process like?

*Make sure you know how much it's going to cost up front and what is expected of you. This will save you time (and money, if you are paying for the consultation) before you visit the office.*

You should know you don't have to pay for the first appointment. Initial consultations with us are free.

Onward...

The consultation can be done in person in one of our many offices, or over the phone. Either way you will get a signed confidentiality agreement before we begin.

First, we will start off by answer any questions you have.

Next, we will determine if your invention even qualifies for a patent or not. To do this we will need to know what the invention his how it works how it's different from other products that are on the market, things of that nature. Do not worry if you don't know the science, or technical ways to make your invention a reality, we are all engineers at the firm so we can quickly understand almost any technical concepts.

If we determine that it is patentable material, we will then provide you with a fixed fee quote for moving forward to the next step. This is a no obligation quote.

Go to www.inventionprep.com to learn how to start profiting off your idea in the next 30 days.

You can decide to retain our firm, or you don't have to. The choice is yours.

Either way you will know if your invention even qualifies for a patent or not, the best strategy for getting protection for your idea, and exact dollar amount for moving to the next step.

Go to www.inventionprep.com to learn how to start profiting off your idea in the next 30 days.

**Question #22: What's the difference between a confidentiality agreement (also known as a non-disclosure agreement) and a patent?**

*This is another option for the inventor. And may make sense in some situations. The attorney should be able to explain when.*

The main difference between a confidentiality agreement and patent is that a patent is property, you own it. A confidentiality agreement is simply a contract between two people.

Allow me to illustrate the limitations of a confidentiality agreement compared to a patent. Let's say you sign a confidentiality agreement with Frank. If Frank steals your idea than you can sue him for breach of contract. However, if Frank tells his brother Fred your idea and Fred goes out and sells it, there's not much you can do. There is no paper trail connecting you to Fred. He did not sign a confidentiality agreement, so you cannot sue him.

However, if you own a patent, it doesn't matter if someone knowingly or unknowingly steals your idea. They are still violating your property rights. Remember confidentiality agreements are contracts and they are governed by contract law. Patents are intellectual property and they are governed by patent law.

Go to www.inventionprep.com to learn how to start profiting off your idea in the next 30 days.

### Question #23: Do I need to set up a company before patenting my idea?

*You can if you want to but it is not necessary. Here's what the attorney should tell you.*

A patent is nothing more than property. Like owning a car or a house. That means it can be owned by you or it could be owned by an entity like a company. So no, you do not have to start an LLC and S corp or any other type of company if you only need to get a patent.

However if you are going to split ownership of the patent between two or more people than you may want to consider starting a company. What you can do then is have the company own the patent and then you share shares in the company with the two or three people. And you can split this ownership up any way you see fit (for example, one of you can own 60%, one can own 20%, and the final person can own 20%, or however you break up the percentages.

Remember, the big reason why people start companies is because it separates their personal liability from their business liability. It has nothing to do with the actual patent process itself.

Go to www.inventionprep.com to learn how to start profiting off your idea in the next 30 days.

**Question #24: Do I need a prototype to patent my idea?**

*You have to explain how the thing would be built in an application, but you don't necessarily need a prototype.*

No. The patent office only requires 3 things to review your idea. First they need a written application. Second they need drawings. Third they need their application fee. That's it. No prototype, business plan, articles of incorporation, plan for manufacturing, or anything of that nature. Just written application, drawings, and application fee.

Go to www.inventionprep.com to learn how to start profiting off your idea in the next 30 days.

## Question #25: I don't have money to patent my idea, do you provide financing options?

*In most cases, the patent application can be broken up into 4 payments over the course of the year. Keep in mind, most of the time the application runs anywhere from $3,000 to $30,000 dollars.*

**Question #26: I'd like to read up about the process some more, do you have any free information I can look at?**

*An attorney should have information about themselves on a website, or something they can mail to you.*

**Question #27: After the idea is patented, do you do anything else to help bring my product to market (like engineering, manufacturing, or marketing)?**

*Some attorneys can point you in the right direction to getting other parts of your idea handled. Most attorneys steer clear of this. A typical response is...*

We can point you in the right direction. But no, we only focus on the legal aspects...making sure your idea is 100% legally protected.

Keep in mind, there are lots of steps when it comes to bringing a product to market.

The first step is usually legal protection with a patent. Next, you have the engineering side which is figuring out how it is going to work, the materials, how it will be made, etc. After that, you may have distribution, retail, accounting the list can go on and on depending on what it is you are inventing.

The key thing to remember here is we are specialists. We work strictly on helping protect your product with a patent. And although we also hold degrees in engineering we do not claim to be experts in those fields. However once we have finished getting you legal protection for your idea we will point you in the right direction to someone who can help you out on the rest of your journey.

Go to www.inventionprep.com to learn how to start profiting off your idea in the next 30 days.

Go to www.inventionprep.com to learn how to
start profiting off your idea in the next 30 days.

# Other common questions:

**Can you help me find venture capital?**

See my response to the question: **After the idea is patented, do you do anything else to help bring my product to market (like engineering, manufacturing, or marketing)?**

**How can I trust you?**

See questions "**How do I know you are not going to steal my idea?**"

**When will my idea be protected?**

See question on "What does patent pending mean?" and question on "How long does it take to get the application submitted?"

**How do I know you will draft the patent application properly?**

See question "How do I know you are not going to steal my idea?" for our experience and track record.

Go to www.inventionprep.com to learn how to start profiting off your idea in the next 30 days.

# How do you find a trustworthy patent attorney?

There are a TON of steps involved in making your dream a reality. From patent protection, to design and engineering, to marketing your idea...and much more.

That's where I come in. I help people who have ideas and inventions (just like you) find the right people to help them out.

I can also show you:

- How to save thousands of dollars on legal fees while patenting your invention

- How to find designers and engineers to create your ideas on paper and in real life (from sketches to prototypes, to mass manufacturing) quicker than you ever dreamed possible

- And, how to get all the money you need WITHOUT investors...usually within 30 days (AND you get to keep ALL your equity)

Most people think it takes a major investment of time and money to get their ideas off the ground.

Now you can start profiting from your ideas and inventions in as little as 30 days.

Go to www.inventionprep.com to learn how to start profiting off your idea in the next 30 days.

If you'd like me to help, just send an email to
Rob@inventionprep.com and we'll take it from there.

Go to www.inventionprep.com to learn how to
start profiting off your idea in the next 30 days.

## Awesome Free Bonuses!

Visit www.inventionprep.com for free instant access to more free cool stuff like...

- Personal feedback from licensed patent professionals, engineers, and experienced marketers on how to protect, create, and sell your idea.
- How to save thousands on legal fees to protect your idea
- Quickly and cheaply create prototypes and final products (in days instead of weeks or months)
- Profit from your idea as quick as humanely possible…usually inside 30 days

Just go to www.inventionprep.com for instant access.

Go to www.inventionprep.com to learn how to start profiting off your idea in the next 30 days.